Sports Build Character

RESPECT IN SPORTS

by Todd Kortemeier

FOCUS READERS

www.focusreaders.com

Focus Readers is distributed by North Star Editions:
sales@northstareditions.com | 888-417-0195

Produced for Focus Readers by Red Line Editorial.

Photographs ©: YakobchukOlena/iStockphoto, cover, 1; aabejon/iStockphoto, 4–5; FlairImages/iStockphoto, 7; Seth Wenig/AP Images, 8–9; David Hahn/Icon SMI CID/Newscom, 11; Elise Amendola/AP Images, 12, 15; Gustavo Garello/AP Images, 16; Fernando Vergara/AP Images, 19; Jan-Philipp Strobel/picture-alliance/dpa/AP Images, 20; kdow/iStockphoto, 22–23, 29; Wavebreakmedia/iStockphoto, 25; mediaphotos/iStockphoto, 26–27

ISBN
978-1-63517-534-9 (hardcover)
978-1-63517-606-3 (paperback)
978-1-63517-750-3 (ebook pdf)
978-1-63517-678-0 (hosted ebook)

Library of Congress Control Number: 2017948104

Printed in the United States of America
Mankato, MN
November, 2017

About the Author

Todd Kortemeier is a writer and editor from Minneapolis. He has written more than 50 books for young people, primarily on sports topics.

TABLE OF CONTENTS

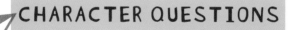

CHAPTER 1

WHAT IS RESPECT?

Respect means being kind to others. But there is more to it than that. It means recognizing that everyone has **value**. In sports, every position is important. The same can also be said for life.

 Teams respect the results of a game by giving high fives.

All people are important. And they should be treated that way.

The goal in sports is to beat the opponent. But that's no reason to treat an opponent without respect. In fact, respect is a key part of being a good sport. Nobody wants to be insulted when they compete. Athletes may be wearing different

LET'S DISCUSS

When was a time someone showed you respect?

 Teammates show respect by cheering for one another.

uniforms. But they should support and respect one another.

Respect makes for a good, clean game. Players can focus on doing their best. And that helps everybody have a good time.

CHAPTER 2

RESPECT IN ACTION

A National Hockey League (NHL) playoff series can last up to seven games. And hockey is a rough sport. Players get battered and bruised. They often crash into one another as they battle for the **puck**.

NHL player Derek Stepan skates off the ice after being injured.

Players put their roughness aside after the series ends. They line up and shake hands on the ice. The players may have been enemies while playing. But they still have respect for one another.

In 2014, the Montreal Canadiens were playing the New York Rangers. Brandon Prust of the Canadiens hit

LET'S DISCUSS

How would it feel to shake an opponent's hand if you had lost?

The Canadiens and Rangers shake hands after the last game in the 2014 series.

Derek Stepan of the Rangers with a **check**. The check broke Stepan's jaw. Still, both men shook hands and wished each other well after the series.

Derek Jeter hits a single in the last game of his career.

The New York Yankees and
Boston Red Sox are two of the best
teams in baseball history. They are

also fierce **rivals**. The two teams have played each other more than 2,000 times. Both teams have passionate fans.

Derek Jeter played for the Yankees from 1995 to 2014. During that time, he became one of the best players in baseball. Of course, Red Sox fans didn't like him. He helped the Yankees win.

In 2014, Jeter announced he was retiring. Other teams honored him in his last visit to their stadiums.

But Jeter didn't know how Red Sox fans would react.

Jeter got a hit in the third inning. The Yankees' **manager** then took Jeter out of the game. He wanted Jeter's career to end on a good note. As Jeter jogged off the field, the crowd roared. They gave him a

LET'S DISCUSS

Can you think of times it might be hard to show respect?

 Jeter waves to cheering fans during his final game.

standing **ovation**. Red Sox players joined in, too.

Jeter spent many years helping the Yankees beat the Red Sox. But Boston fans respected him for being a great player.

SUDAMERICANA 2016

▷ **Chapecoense players posed for a picture less than a month before their plane crashed.**

In 2016, Chapecoense was living a dream. The Brazilian soccer team was one of the country's smallest clubs. They rarely challenged for a title. But 2016 was different. They were competing in a South American tournament. They had made it to the final. It was the biggest match in team history.

But tragedy struck on the way. The team's plane crashed. Almost the whole team was on board. Seventy people died. Nineteen of them were Chapecoense players.

Chapecoense could not go on. They did not have enough players.

They didn't have the desire to play, either. They would have to **forfeit** to Colombia's Atletico Nacional.

Clubs around the world mourned for Chapecoense. So did Atletico Nacional. Atletico refused to accept the title because of the tragedy. They insisted it be given to Chapecoense.

Atletico received the **FIFA** Fair Play Award for showing good sportsmanship. Their action didn't erase what happened. But

 Atletico Nacional fans hold the Brazilian and Colombian flags to pay their respects.

the respect they showed was a

kind gesture.

 Elana Meyers won second place in the first World Cup race of 2014.

Elana Meyers was a two-time Olympic medalist in bobsled. She arrived early to the 2014 World Cup to get some extra practice. But her US teammates hadn't arrived yet. She needed a **brakeman**.

One day, a member of the US men's team helped her practice.

But the next day, nobody else was available. Then, the Romanian team loaned Meyers one of its brakemen.

Bobsled is a dangerous sport. Athletes can get hurt. It was risky for the Romanian team to help Meyers. But they respected their opponent. They wanted Meyers to have the practice she needed.

LET'S DISCUSS

Why is it important for athletes to show respect to other teams?

CHAPTER 3

RESPECT AND YOU

Athletes play fair by showing others respect. Daily life is no different. Respect makes school, home, and other places feel welcoming. Everyone should feel respected during his or her day.

Athletes show respect by following their coach's instructions.

Respecting teammates and friends can be easy. But people who seem different from you also deserve respect. Respect means treating others as your equals.

In sports, you may not like your opponent. In daily life, you might disagree with others. Respect is not about liking everyone. You can

LET'S DISCUSS

Should you treat someone with respect if they disrespect you? Why or why not?

➤ **Being quiet at the library is one example of respect.**

disagree with someone and still

show respect.

   Respect is a team effort. When

people treat one another with

respect, everybody wins.

ARE YOU RESPECTFUL?

Ask yourself these questions and decide.

- Do I listen when others are speaking?
- Do I raise my hand in class?
- Do I use kind words when I speak?
- Do I think before I act?
- Am I polite toward others?

It feels good to respect others. It also feels good to respect yourself. Challenge yourself today to do both. You could say thank-you to a teacher. You could also notice something you're good at.

Raising your hand shows your teacher respect.

FOCUS ON
RESPECT

Write your answers on a separate piece of paper.

1. Write a sentence that summarizes how Atletico Nacional showed respect in Chapter 2.

2. Who is your favorite athlete who's not on your favorite team? What do you respect about this athlete?

3. Which team is the rival of the Boston Red Sox?
   A. the New York Rangers
   B. the New York Yankees
   C. the Montreal Canadiens

4. Why was it risky for Romania to loan Elana Meyers an athlete?
   A. The athlete could have injured herself during practice.
   B. Meyers could have learned about Romanian strategy.
   C. Other teams could have also asked Romania for help.

5. What does **battered** mean in this book?

*Players get **battered** and bruised. They often crash into one another as they battle for the puck.*

    A. tired

    B. scared

    C. injured

6. What does **roared** mean in this book?

*As Jeter jogged off the field, the crowd **roared**. They gave him a standing ovation.*

    A. left their seats

    B. cheered loudly

    C. shouted angrily

Answer key on page 32.

GLOSSARY

brakeman
The athlete in a bobsled who pulls the brakes at the end of a race.

check
When one player uses his or her body to hit another player.

FIFA
The organization in charge of international soccer.

forfeit
When a team is forced to give their opponent a victory without playing.

manager
A baseball team's head coach.

ovation
A show of appreciation, such as cheering or clapping.

puck
The small rubber disk that hockey players try to hit into the net.

rivals
Teams or players that have an intense and ongoing competition against one another.

uniforms
Matching clothes that members of a team wear.

value
Worth or importance.

TO LEARN MORE

BOOKS

Herzog, Brad. *Inspiring Stories of Sportsmanship*. Minneapolis: Free Spirit Publishing, 2014.

Raatma, Lucia. *Respect*. Ann Arbor, MI: Cherry Lake Publishing, 2014.

Sundem, Garth. *Real Kids, Real Stories, Real Character: Choices That Matter around the World*. Minneapolis: Free Spirit Publishing, 2016.

NOTE TO EDUCATORS

Visit **www.focusreaders.com** to find lesson plans, activities, links, and other resources related to this title.

INDEX

Answer Key: 1. Answers will vary; **2.** Answers will vary; **3.** B; **4.** A; **5.** C; **6.** B